Alter, Judy,
1938-

5   Th

THE COMANCHES

JUDY ALTER

THE COMANCHES

Franklin Watts   New York   Chicago   London   Toronto   Sydney   A First Book

Map by Joe LeMonnier

Cover photograph copyright © Photo Researchers Inc./Museum of the
American Indian/Tom McHugh

Photographs copyright ©: Photo Researchers Inc.: pp. 3 (Peter B. Kaplan),
11 (Marvin B. Winter), 16 (Museum of the American Indian/Tom
McHugh); New York Public Library, Picture Collection: pp. 14, 27; North
Wind Picture Archives, Alfred, Me.: pp. 18, 23, 25, 35, 37, 43; Museum
of the Great Plains, Lawton, Oklahoma: pp. 20, 30, 39, 41, 48, 53, 55,
57; Stock Montage/Historical Pictures, Chicago, Il.: p. 24; Panhandle-
Plains Historical Museum, Canyon, Texas: p.51.

Library of Congress Cataloging-in-Publication Data

Alter, Judy, 1938–
The Comanches / Judy Alter.
p. cm. — (A First Book)
Includes bibliographical references (p.   ) and index.
ISBN 0-531-20115-5 (hrd cover). — ISBN 0-531-15683-4 (trd pbk)
1. Comanche Indians—History—Juvenile literature. 2. Comanche
Indians—Social life and customs—Juvenile literature.
[1. Comanche Indians. 2. Indians of North America.] I. Title.
II. Series.
E99.C85A47   1994
973'.04974—dc20   93-23265   CIP   AC

CONTENTS

THE COMANCHES

COMANCHES, HORSES, AND TERRITORY

They called themselves The People. Neighboring Indian peoples, with whom they were often at war, called them Comanches, a word meaning "enemy" or "anyone who wants to fight all the time," in the words of the Ute Indians. The tribe was first known in the area we now call Wyoming, where they, like their cousins the Utes, were part of the Shoshone nation. Not much is known about the Comanches' early history, except that they had no horses to hunt buffalo and antelope, they lived mostly on berries, fruit, and small game, and they were a poor tribe that did not move around a great deal. When they did move a village, they used dogs as pack animals.

Various stories account for the split between the Shoshones and the Comanches — perhaps a hunting dispute or the coming of a terrible disease. Whatever the cause, the Comanches moved south. They were first seen by Spaniards in the Southwest in 1705, when they accompanied their kinsmen, the Utes, to Taos to trade. By then, the various bands of the tribe were living in the land between what is now southern Colorado and western Kansas. The landscape in this great territory varied, but much of it was prairie with lush thick grass that supported countless buffalo, elk, deer, and antelope.

The Comanches first got horses from the Utes, who taught them to ride. Then they acquired them from the Spaniards, either by barter or raiding. Having horses changed life dramatically for the Comanches, giving them the freedom to roam the Plains and the ability to develop great skill as warriors and buffalo hunters. On horseback, they could travel greater distances to find buffalo for food, and the tribe, no longer confined to a limited diet, became healthier and grew in numbers. Within a generation of their acquiring horses, the Comanches became the most skilled horsemen of the Plains, and nobody could beat them when it came to hunting and fighting on horseback.

Horses gave the Comanches a reason to go to war and to raid settlements, for the Comanches always wanted more and better horses.

HORSES WERE AN INTEGRAL PART OF COMANCHE LIFE. HERE A
HUNTER ON HORSEBACK KILLS A BUFFALO.

When American settlers pushed into Comanche territory, principally Texas, southern Colorado, and eastern New Mexico, they called the Comanches "the lords of the Plains." The Comanches were the most fierce warriors, the most skillful and graceful horsemen of the Plains Indians, and the last tribe to submit to reservation life.

By the time the early white settlers discovered the Comanches, around 1800, they found a prosperous and warlike tribe numbering some 5,000 in population, scattered into six separate and distinct divisions, each made up of several bands (or groups) with no central governing council and little unity among them. The various bands ranged the Plains from eastern Colorado and New Mexico to Kansas, Oklahoma, and Texas, a vast land that the Spanish called the *Comancheria*. The major divisions were the Penatekas (Honey-Eaters), who lived in the southern portion of the territory, the Nokonis (Those Who Move Often), the Tenawas and the Tanimas (Liver-Eaters) who lived primarily in North Texas, the Yamparikas (Potato-Eaters), the Kotsotekas (Buffalo-Eaters) of Oklahoma and Kansas, and the Kwahadis (Antelope). The Kwahadis, the band led by the famous Quanah Parker, became the last holdouts from reservation life, taking final refuge in the canyons of the Texas Panhandle.

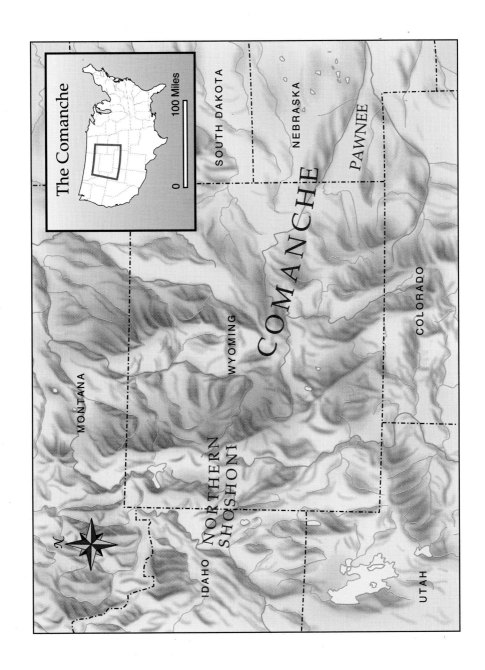

The Comanche

100 Miles

0

SOUTH DAKOTA

NEBRASKA

PAWNEE

COMANCHE

COLORADO

WYOMING

MONTANA

NORTHERN SHOSHONI

IDAHO

UTAH

CHIEF QUANAH PARKER AND HIS WIFE AT THEIR HOME IN INDIAN TERRITORY (LATER THE STATE OF OKLAHOMA) DURING THE 1890S.

Raiding the settlements of their enemies — Mexicans and American settlers alike — and being bribed with presents to stop this kind of raiding had become a way of life for the Comanches. They had also soundly defeated the Apaches, driving them out of their Texas territory and into the mountains of New Mexico and across the Rio Grande into Mexico.

[14]

HUNTING AND FOOD

The horse was wealth to a Comanche, who used it for gifts, trade, and war. But the animal that fed and clothed the tribe was the buffalo. There were millions of buffalo on the Plains, especially in the Great Herd, which was said to be 50 miles (80 km) deep and 25 miles (40 km) wide. Comanches hunted in the summer and fall, when the buffalo hides made the best robes, and the whole village took part in the hunt. Armed with bows and arrows, men on horseback circled a herd, always staying downwind because buffalo had poor sight but a keen sense of smell. Once the kill was made, each hunter skinned and butchered the buffalo he had killed, then packed it on mules and took it back to the village. There the women sliced

BISON HUNT PAINTED ON ELK SKIN, 1800S

the meat for drying and spread out the hide for tanning — it would be used for tepees, clothing, thongs, saddles, bridles, and bags. The *sinews,* or tendons, became bow-strings and thread; the horns and hooves were used for cups, spoons, and ornaments; the paunch, or stomach, was made into a water bag; buffalo hair was twisted into ropes; the dried *buffalo chips,* or droppings, were used for fuel. The raw liver, still warm, was considered a delicacy, and sometimes a triumphant hunter also drank the blood of the buffalo he had just killed. Nothing was wasted.

Comanches also hunted deer, antelope, and black bear, and if food was scarce, they would eat horse meat, but dog meat and human flesh were forbidden. Meat was cooked on a stick over a fire until white traders introduced the use of copper pots. After that, meat was stewed. Comanches also used fruit and vegetables for both food and medicine — persimmons, mulberries, wild plums, grapes, prickly pear cactus, juniper berries, pecans, and some root vegetables, such as wild onions and radishes. They did not have bread, but a favorite food was *pemmican,* made of buffalo meat mixed with wild berries, nuts, and boiled tallow or fat from the buffalo. Packed into a buffalo-hide bag or piece of intestine, pemmican would keep for years.

THE LUSH GRASSES OF THE GREAT PLAINS SUPPORTED A
WIDE VARIETY OF WILDLIFE. HERE A COMANCHE HUNTER
STALKS HIS ANTELOPE PREY.

Food was either scarce or plentiful for the
Comanches. When it was scarce, they ate pemmican
and dried jerky or went hungry, without complaining.
If necessary, on the warpath or a raid, they could go
for hours and hours without food or water.

CLOTHING AND APPEARANCE

Comanches were not the colorful Indians that you see in books, tall and kingly, wearing lots of feathers, beads, and paint. Rather, men wore a *breechclout* that looked almost like a huge diaper and was drawn between the legs and belted with loose flaps hanging down to the knees at both the front and the back. Frequently, moccasins and a breechclout were all that the men wore, although they also had buckskin leggings with long fringes and shirts of deer or antelope hide decorated with fringes (often of scalp hair) and ornaments. A buffalo robe — warmer than four ordinary blankets — protected them in winter, and they had knee-high boots made of buffalo hide with the fur side in. Feathers worn on the head were a sign of distinction, but the Comanches did not have war

MINNIE BLACK-STAR (LEFT) AND TIS-SO-YO (RIGHT) WEAR
TRADITIONAL COMANCHE CLOTHES IN THESE PHOTOGRAPHS
FROM THE NINETEENTH CENTURY.

bonnets — elaborate headdresses often seen in paintings and engravings — until later, when they lived on the reservations.

The men were proud of their hair and kept it greased, a sign of good grooming. They wore it braided, with pieces of silver, tin, or glass on the side of the head as decoration, and they often painted the part on their scalp in red or white. Men wore shell earrings in their pierced ears, and often had six or eight holes in one ear and three or four in the other.

Women were less fussy about their hair, wearing it short and cropped. But they were careful about their makeup, tracing red and yellow lines around their eyes and painting the inside of their ears red. A circle or triangle of red or orange was made on each cheek. The women wore buckskin skirts and poncho-type blouses with beading across the shoulders and down the sleeves. They had beaded moccasins and wore leggings in winter.

Little boys generally went naked in warm weather until they were seven or eight; then they wore a breechclout. Girls wore a breechclout until they were twelve or thirteen.

HOUSING AND WORK

Comanches lived in tepees. It took between ten and seventeen buffalo hides to cover a tepee frame, which was made of twenty or thirty poles of pine or cedar. But such a cone-shaped tepee could shelter as many as twenty people. It had a smoke hole near the top and the opening always faced the rising sun. The tepee repelled wind and water and was warm and dry, a much more comfortable home than the dugouts and shacks of the early white settlers. The hides of the tepee were staked to the ground to keep out drafts, except in summer, when they were rolled up a little to let in air. Sometimes extra hides were used to curtain off private spaces inside the tepee. Because the Comanches moved frequently, tepees were made to be taken down or put up within minutes.

LIKE MANY PLAINS INDIANS, THE COMANCHES LIVED
IN TEPEES MADE FROM BETWEEN TEN AND SEVENTEEN
BUFFALO HIDES.

Comanches were nomadic, traveling around the Plains and never camping for long in any one spot. Their constant moving was probably a result of several things — a need for fresh grass for their hundreds of ponies, and a need for new buffalo herds to hunt, a wish for a clean campsite, and a sense of safety. If the Comanches stayed in one place too long, their enemies might find them. Campsites were chosen for food, shelter, safety, and convenience. At each campsite, tepees were grouped around that of the leader. When it was time to dismantle the tepees, the

TEPEES WERE EASILY DISMANTLED AND MOVED USING HORSES OR DOGS. THE TEPEE POLES NOT ONLY SUPPORTED THE HIDE COVERING BUT ALSO WERE USED IN MAKING THE TRAVOIS.

lodge poles were used to make a *travois*. In addition to personal belongings, an infant or a very elderly or ill person could also be carried on the travois.

Work was clearly divided in a Comanche village. Boys learned to ride early, usually having their own ponies by the time they were four or five; girls were taught to cook and tan hides. The women prepared the food, tanned animal hides, made tepees and clothes, and took care of the children. Men had to be ready to protect the campsite. They also went on raids and hunts, or made weapons. When they weren't doing those things, the men lounged around the village, sleeping and playing. When the band traveled, the women carried the burdens, so the men could be free to protect them if enemies attacked. When the men were away on a raid or a hunt, the women kept busy making moccasins and clothes for their families, making pemmican, and tending to the domestic side of Comanche life.

THIS FREDERIC REMINGTON DRAWING SHOWS A YOUNG BOY BREAKING A PONY. FROM AN EARLY AGE, BOYS WERE TAUGHT THE IMPORTANCE OF HORSES TO THE COMANCHE WAY OF LIFE.

WEAPONS

After his horses, a man's bow was his most prized possession. It was wooden, made of the tree sometimes called *bois d'arc,* or Osage orange, with a string made of firm gut. Arrows were made of seasoned polished wood with bone or flint tips and feathers to give them flight and accuracy. Because it took special skill and a lot of time to make arrows that were lightweight, straight, and well balanced, a hunter would often search to recover arrows he had shot. The bow and arrow was actually a better weapon than early muskets — it could be reloaded more quickly and was more accurate. Comanches had no use for firearms until repeating rifles and six-shooters were introduced.

In battle, men carried a shield made from the shoulder hide of an old buffalo bull because it was

THE COMANCHES' WEAPONS, BESIDES THEIR HORSES,
INCLUDED BOWS, ARROWS, AND SHIELDS MADE FROM
THICK BUFFALO HIDES.

tougher than the hide of younger animals. The hide was heated and steamed to shrink and toughen it. Layers of hide were padded with feathers or hair, then sewn over a wooden hoop. Next, the shield was dried or cured. The outside of the shield was curved to turn away arrows, and was decorated with bear teeth, scalps, or the tails of horses and mules. For a warrior, the shield was spiritual as well as physical protection.

Both the lance and battle-ax were also used in war. The battle-ax, or war club, was made of a wedge of sharpened flint stone tied with rawhide to a wooden handle. The lance was the most dangerous weapon, because it was never thrown but used in hand-to-hand combat. When a lance was used in battle, there were only two possible outcomes — victory or death — and only the bravest of warriors carried lances.

CHILDREN

Comanches were sociable Indians. They liked to visit and dance and feast. Many nights, they sat around their fires, listening to the old men tell stories that were both entertainment and education for the young ones. They also liked to play ball games such as *lacrosse,* and they had their own team games, such as *shinny* and double ball, which may be like versions of soccer. Comanches were also great gamblers.

The Comanches valued their children highly, although the boys were preferred. Infants were bound into *cradleboards* for the first few months of their life and then carried on their mothers' backs until they were able to walk. Comanches had no last names, such as Smith or Jones, so children were called by pet names. When they were old enough a public naming ceremony gave them a formal name,

COMANCHE INFANTS WERE CARRIED ON
THEIR MOTHERS' BACKS.

usually one based on an event or circumstance. Typical Comanche names, translated into English, were Ten Bears, Bull Bear, and Silver Knife.

When boys and girls were old enough to court, their behavior was governed by strict rules. They could not show any interest while in the camp, although there were often lots of secret meetings. When a young man wanted a wife and the girl was willing, he gave her family a horse — or several horses if he was wealthy and considered her a prize. This was not a purchase price but a way of showing that he would be a good provider. It was not uncommon for a warrior to have more than one wife, but the first wife was always the boss of the others. A second wife was usually a younger sister to the first, because sisters were unlikely to quarrel. Arranged marriages between a young girl and an older man were common, but marriages could be dissolved for any number of reasons. When young men married, they lived with their wifes' families. To keep the peace, the husbands never spoke directly to their mothers-in-law.

For Comanche youths, stealing horses from enemy tribes was dangerous but rewarding. Successful raiders were honored and wealthy. Four or five young men would follow a leader, traveling on foot at night until they were deep in enemy hunting grounds. When they found an enemy camp, the scary part began. They stole into camp in the middle of the night, because the best war ponies and buffalo runners were always tied next to their owners' tepees at night. The raiders had to cut the ropes and lead the horses away without waking their owners. To do this, they led the animals a few steps and stopped, keeping this up until they were out of hearing. Then they would mount the ponies and race for their lives. If, on the other hand, they had led the ponies straight out of camp, the sleeping warriors would have heard the steady walk of the horse and awakened instantly. This way, the occasional sounds seemed like the stamping of horses tied up for the night. The Comanches were the most skillful of all the Plains tribes at stealing horses.

WAR

War was as important if not more so than stealing horses. Comanches sometimes went to war just for the prestige it brought them, but more often for revenge. In the end, they fought to keep the white settlers out of *Comancheria*. Men centered their lives around war and gained social rank by their brave battle deeds. "Counting coup" brought a warrior honor and fame — *coup* is a French word, meaning "blow." Counting coup meant striking a blow against an enemy, and coups were rated according to the degree of skill and danger involved. A man did not need to kill his enemy to count coup. Striking a live enemy with a lance or *coup stick* was the highest coup because it took more bravery than shooting an arrow from a distance. Scalping a downed enemy was not particularly honorable — in the Comanche view, anyone could scalp a dead enemy. But if it were done in dangerous circumstances, then it was counting coup. To lie about coup meant bad luck, even death. The Comanches valued bravery above everything else.

White settlers pushing into *Comancheria* did not understand that, in their way, the Comanches were religious people, though theirs was not a tightly organized religion. The Comanches believed in a Great Spirit, which brought good, and an Evil Spirit, which accounted for disasters. According to their story of creation, the Great Spirit created the Comanche people after destroying a previous, unsatisfactory people by flood. The Great Spirit was in various ways linked to the sun, the moon, and the earth. Comanches saw spirits in the animals and objects of the natural world — sun, earth, rivers, hills, buffalo, deer, eagles, and other things of nature, both living and inanimate. These spirits had the power to bring them success in hunting or battle, to keep the tribe safe, and bring it a plentiful supply of food. Elaborate ceremonies were held to keep the Comanches in favor with the spirits. A War Dance was always held the night before the men went into battle or on a raid. To hold the dance in the day was bad luck.

Comanches raided in the night just after a full moon, which came to be called a Comanche Moon. With bloodcurdling yells and cries, they encircled an enemy, drawing the circle ever smaller. When close enough to the enemy, a warrior would slip sideways into a loop around his horse's neck and shoot arrows from beneath the neck of his racing horse. The animal thus protected the warrior, but it took great skill to shoot accurately from that position — and on a galloping horse!

ARTIST FREDERIC REMINGTON CAPTURED THE DRAMA OF A WARRIOR SHOOTING FROM BENEATH THE NECK OF HIS HORSE.

White people thought that the Comanches were among the most savage of enemies because they usually killed the men they captured and took women and children as prisoners, sometimes treating them cruelly. If weak or very young captives slowed the Indians down during their flight from a battle, they killed the captives. But the Indians did not know the white man's code of war and were governed by their own. They were brave and courageous and admired those traits in others, including whites. If captives showed courage, they were sometimes adopted into a tribe and became honored members because of the value Comanches placed on bravery.

If a warrior was killed, the entire camp grieved when the war party returned. New captives might be killed in revenge; women cut their hair and gashed their arms and legs; sometimes they cut off their fingertips.

But when a successful war or raiding party returned in victory, there was a great celebration. Warriors painted their faces black as a sign of victory and then waited until morning to ride into camp, so that everyone could see them. The women relatives would praise them loudly, making them the center of attention, and there was often a Victory Dance.

IN ADDITION TO MOVING THEIR BELONGINGS, THE COMANCHES
OFTEN USED TRAVOIS TO MOVE THE AGED OR WOUNDED.

WHITE SETTLERS ARRIVE

The Comanches were always at war with their neighbors, except for the Kiowas, who lived with them. In the north, they fought the Pawnees; to the south, they raided the Spanish; on the plains, they battled the Cheyennes and drove the Apaches south and west. But by the 1830s, the Comanches considered whites their real enemy. They had defeated the Spanish and the Apaches before, but there had never been so many of them. To the Comanches, it must have seemed that there was an unending number of white settlers coming to the Southwest.

These settlers kept moving farther into the *Comancheria*, the land the Comanches considered their own. Without understanding that they were invading the Indians' territory, the settlers built lonely

A RESTORATION OF FORT PARKER AT
GROESBECK, TEXAS

cabins without neighbors or defenses. Because these invaders often had better horses than the Indians', the Comanches were tempted to raid their lonely cabins. From the 1830s, Comanche history is a story told in battles with the white settlers, the U.S. Army, and the government.

The first major clash between the two peoples was the raid by the Comanches on Parker's Fort in Central Texas in 1836. Thirty-four people, half of them children, lived in this stockade, but only five or six men were present on the spring morning that the Comanches, with some Kiowas, appeared. After pretending to be friendly, the Indians attacked the fort, killed many people — a few escaped — and took five captives, including a woman named Rachel Plummer, whose written account of her captivity later made many whites condemn the "savage" Comanches. Also taken prisoner was nine-year-old Cynthia Parker.

Cynthia Ann Parker is one of the most famous of all captives taken by Indians. Because she showed great bravery, the Comanches adopted her. She lived with them for twenty-four years, grew up thinking of herself as a Comanche, and married a chief of the Antelope (or Kwahadi) band, Peta Nocona. Their son, Quanah Parker, was the chief who held out longest against the whites but also the one who finally encouraged his people to accept reservation life. In

1860, Texas Ranger Sul Ross defeated a band of Indians under Peta Nocona and captured Cynthia Ann. Ross thought she was an Indian until he saw her blue eyes. Cynthia Ann and her daughter, Prairie Flower, were returned to the Parker family, but she mourned for her husband and her son, whose fate she did not know. When Prairie Flower died of disease,

Cynthia Ann died soon after, of a broken heart, most people said. Several novels and short stories have been written about Cynthia Ann Parker.

The Indians continued to raid and take captives. Treaties were made and broken on both sides, and the Texas Rangers, then newly formed, were often sent to retaliate for Comanche attacks on settlements. But after an Indian camp was attacked in 1831, the Penateka Comanches requested a council to make peace. An exchange of prisoners was agreed upon. For the council, sixty-five men, women, and children of a Penateka band came to San Antonio in 1840 with many ponies and buffalo hides. The fact that they had brought women and children would later show they were not expecting trouble. But then the Comanches had no reason to expect trouble. They had been invited to this meeting and, to Comanches, hospitality was sacred — even the most bitter enemy could not be harmed if he was an invited guest.

They brought only one captive, fourteen-year-old Matilda Lockhart. According to some stories, Matilda later told the authorities in San Antonio that the Comanches planned to get as high a ransom for her as possible and then return the other captives, one by one, each time getting a good price. It is possible, though, that she was the only captive held by the Penateka band. Because each band was independent,

A COUNCIL OF WAR

it actually had no control over the captives held by other bands of Comanches — a fact that the white men in San Antonio did not understand.

When the Comanches were in the Council House for the meeting to which they had been invited, the white men became angered. The Indians had not brought as many captives as had been expected and the Lockhart girl had apparently been badly mistreated, so they surrounded the Indians and told them they would be held hostage until all captives were returned. The Comanches were indignant that they, as invited guests, were treated in such an inhospitable manner.

The Council House fight was on, and when it was over, seven Texans, and thirty-five Comanches, including the chiefs, were killed in a fight that raged through the streets of San Antonio and even into some private homes. The remaining Indians were imprisoned, and one woman was sent to deliver a warning to her tribe to return the rest of the captives. Instead, the Indians killed the captives.

In retaliation for the Council House fight, several hundred Comanches led a raid south in Texas, stealing and killing as they went and finally burning the Gulf Coast town of Linnville. The residents escaped only by taking to boats, where the Indians could not —or would not — follow. The retreating Indians were followed by a large posse and soundly defeated in the

Battle of Plum Creek. Feeling the Comanches still had not been punished strongly enough, the people of Texas ordered an attack on an Indian village to the north. More than one hundred Comanche men were killed in the surprise raid on the sleeping village; women, children, and horses were captured.

From 1840 until the Civil War, the Comanches' way of life was pressured by the great migrations of settlers who came in waves with the 1849 gold strike in California and the 1859 discovery of gold in Colorado, by Indian tribes from the East who were displaced by westward-advancing settlers, and by the diseases brought by the settlers — smallpox, cholera, syphilis, and alcoholism. Buffalo hunters began depleting the great herds that had been the Indians' source of food, shelter, and most of the necessities of life. For all these reasons, poverty and hunger increased among the Comanches and, as desperation grew, so did their raids on white settlements and deep into Mexico, where they nearly depopulated the northern part of the country. Treaties were made, presents given, brief periods of peace established, only to be broken. Then the raiding was renewed.

The Comanches distrusted the whites after so many broken promises, including the treachery of the Council House fight, and the only treaty condition that would satisfy them was an impossible one: no more settlers in the *Comancheria*. But the Comanches were not the easiest people with whom to make a treaty. For one thing, the white men could never get all the roaming bands of Comanches together to make a treaty. Whites would sign a treaty with one band, only to be attacked by another that had made no treaty. The white men did not understand the difference between these bands of Comanches and simply thought the Indians were breaking their treaties. The whites would then attack, but they would never know if they were attacking the Indians who staged the latest raid or another group. When warriors did sign treaties, they came to meetings only when it suited them, and though the older chiefs were in favor of peace, they could not control the angry young warriors. The raiding continued.

By the outbreak of the Civil War, the Comanches were desperate. And then, the attention of the army was on the war, not the Plains Indians. The Comanches signed treaties with both the Union and the Confederacy as it suited their convenience, but felt no loyalty to either side. Neither army could spare men to fight the Indians, so the Comanches used this time to increase their raiding — they were principally interested in stealing horses, but without hesitation killed those settlers who got in the way of their horse-stealing encounters.

AFTER THE CIVIL WAR

From the close of the Civil War on, the history of the Comanches is difficult to separate from that of other tribes of Plains Indians, principally the Kiowas and the southern Cheyennes. In 1867, the major Indian tribes of the southern Plains — Comanche, Cheyenne, Arapaho, Kiowa, and Kiowa-Apache — signed the treaty of Medicine Lodge, which gave them all the things they didn't want: houses, farm tools, and military posts. They were confined to a reservation of two million acres (800,000 hectares) of beautiful country but were allowed to leave it to hunt buffalo in west Texas. Ten Bears, who spoke for the Comanches, said that his people had not started the difficulty, and that they held firm to their right to their land and their resistance to being held prisoner

CHIEF TEN BEARS

within the walls and fences of a reservation. But the Comanches, and the other tribes, signed the treaty. The best guess is that the Indians never planned to stay on the reservation. As long as game was plentiful and they could get rifles from traders, most Indians would stay off the reservation.

Efforts to teach farming to the few Indians on the reservation were unsuccessful. Men who were warriors and hunters did not take easily to the hard work of farming. The government took their land, they said, so let the government feed them. They became even less interested in farming after some of them ate some green watermelons they had stolen, causing what one Indian described as "Devil inside my belly."

In midwinter of 1868, General George Armstrong Custer led a massacre of peaceful Cheyennes of Black Kettle's band, who were camped on the Washita River in Oklahoma. After this unprovoked attack, the Plains Indians were convinced that the government's promises were unreliable. But increasing attacks by the army — and several major defeats for the Indians — forced many to try the "white man's road." Some Comanche bands were among those seeking peace. Satanta, a Kiowa leader, spoke for those who stayed off the reservation when he called the white man's road hard, saying it had nothing on it but corn, which hurt the Indians' teeth.

The Kwahadi, or Antelope band, of southern Comanches, led by Quanah Parker, the son of the captive Cynthia Ann Parker, were fierce holdouts from reservation life; they retreated to the Staked Plains, or Llano Estacado, in the Panhandle of Texas, where they could hunt in freedom. They traded robes, captives, and stolen cattle for rifles, ammunition, calico, and geegaws with the Comancheros, traders from the New Mexico settlements. Among the Kwahadi, a leader called Isatai became prominent. A medicine man thought to have supernatural powers, Isatai preached war, claimed to have spoken with the Great Spirit and to have brought the dead back to life, and said no bullet could ever harm him. To convince his fellow tribesmen, he swallowed rifle cartridges.

Isatai did something no other Comanche had been able to do: he drew together all the scattered bands still outside the reservation. Then the Comanches held their very first Sun Dance. This dance was an annual ceremony for the Kiowas, and the Comanches had seen it. Now, to gather power for an attack on the white people, they borrowed the ceremony and turned it into a war dance. Then they attacked a group of white buffalo hunters headquartered in an old trading post, known as Adobe Walls, in the Texas Panhandle. The Comanches were particularly angry about the buffalo hunters who killed ani-

MEDICINE MAN ISATAI (FRONT) IN A
FAMILY PORTRAIT

mals by the thousands, skinned them, and then left their carcasses to rot or feed wolves and vultures. To the Indians, who used every part of the buffalo, this waste was a terrible offense to nature. The Comanches could not foresee the worst of it — that the buffalo hunters would kill all the buffalo.

Twenty-six men and one woman lived at Adobe Walls, and they had something the Indians hadn't counted on — buffalo guns that were accurate at a long distance and that fired large bullets. One Comanche said, "White man's gun shoot today, kill tomorrow." Holed up inside the trading post, the hunters not only held off the Indians but killed many. In addition, the Indians were poorly organized, relying only on Isatai's inspiration. Their attack failed and for several days they could do no more than keep the hunters pinned inside the fort. Isatai was disgraced when his horse was shot from under him, and he had to be rescued. Finally, the Indians retreated.

The U.S. Army responded to the Battle of Adobe Walls by sending out the greatest concentration of troops ever mounted against the Indians. In defeat, more bands entered the reservation. But still the Kwahadi Comanches held out, with bands of Kiowas and southern Cheyennes.

In September 1874, troops under the command of Colonel Ranald Mackenzie surprised the sleeping Indians in the Palo Duro Canyon of the

Texas Panhandle. Few Indians were killed or captured, but their tepees and food supplies were destroyed, and their entire herd of horses was killed — Mackenzie had learned to kill the horses rather than keep them for the Indians to steal back. Winter was coming, and the Kwahadis had no horses for hunting, or supplies to feed and clothe their families. After a miserable winter during which many Indians died, Quanah Parker led the Kwahadis to the reservation at Fort Sill, Oklahoma. In August 1875, a count showed just under 1,600 Comanches on the reservation—all that was left of a once-proud tribe of 5,000.

THE AREA AROUND FORT SILL, OKLAHOMA, BECAME THE NEW RESERVATION HOME FOR QUANAH PARKER AND HIS PEOPLE.

RESERVATION LIFE

Because the reservation was too small to allow them to roam and hunt as they formerly had, many Comanches did not care if they lived or died. They could not provide their own food and were given rations of beef, cornmeal, sugar, coffee, and soap. But the rations were often skimpy and not of good quality. The Comanches detested cornmeal and fed it to their horses, but gradually they learned to eat the grain, vegetables, and bread. When the Indian agent had no food for them, they ate their ponies to keep from starving.

Clothes were another problem. The government issued a suit of clothing — shirt, pants, coat, hat, and socks — to every male over fourteen years of age, and to every female over twelve, one woolen skirt, 12 yards (11 m) each of calico and homespun cloth, and one pair of woolen hose. The poorly made

COMANCHES AWAIT THE DISTRIBUTION OF RATIONS
AT FORT SILL AGENCY, OKLAHOMA

suits were all of the same size, made to fit a 200-pound (90 kg) man. The shirts were made of red flannel, and the hats were tall stovepipes, like the one Abraham Lincoln wore. The Indians cut up the suits into leggings and vests, using the cast-off parts to clothe the children; women wrapped the calico around themselves, not knowing how to sew it.

Comanche children were sent to schools run by missionaries and other white men, schools designed to teach them to live like white people and abandon their tribal heritage. Comanches felt the old way of life slipping farther and farther away.

Small groups of Comanches left the reservation every year, with government permission, for the annual buffalo hunt. But in 1878, they could find no buffalo. The elders believed that the buffalo would come with winter and waited; when the herd did not appear, they realized finally that the buffalo were gone — the white hide-hunters had killed them all. Gone, too, with the buffalo, was the old way of life. Barbed-wire fences and railroad tracks crisscrossed the land, and cowboys and Texas Rangers now rode where the Comanches had once roamed free.

In the following years, Quanah Parker did a masterful job of helping his people adjust to the white man's road. He became a successful rancher, leased pasture to Texas cattlemen, was a judge of the Indian Court and a recognized leader of all the bands of Comanches. Eventually, Quanah and his several wives and many children lived in a huge, two-story, white frame house at Cache, Oklahoma; with big stars painted on its roof, it was called the Comanche White House by some people.

In the 1890s, with the Oklahoma land boom, the gradual whittling away of the Comanches' land began, in spite of their protests. Settlers demanded that the government open more and more Indian lands for homesteading, arguing that the lands were not being used as well as they could be. Finally, the government allotted 160 acres (64 hectares) of land to each Indian

THE BRUSH ARBOR SHELTER PROVIDED RELIEF FROM THE HARSH OKLAHOMA SUMMER SUN FOR THIS COMANCHE FAMILY.

man, woman, and child, set aside a few tracts of land for the Indians collectively, and opened the rest of the reservation for settlement. The Indians were to be paid two million dollars. Towns such as Anadarko and Lawton sprang up overnight, and settlers in wagons and traders on horseback filled the Indians' land.

By the late 1890s, most Comanches had established farms and were raising cattle. They also earned money by leasing grazing land to Texas ranchers and by doing odd jobs, probably for settlers, now that they lived in a populated area. By 1907, when Oklahoma became a state, reservation life was a thing of the past. It had lasted only forty years.

Today, some Comanches have lost their tribal identity through marriage or moving to cities, but many still live in Texas and Oklahoma and hold onto their heritage with pride, recounting tribal history to youngsters and following the ways of the past whenever possible. For example, in Fort Worth, Texas, in September 1990, descendants of Chief Quanah Parker and other Comanches joined in a powwow, or traditional dance competition, in honor of the legendary hero. Following ancient custom, a medicine man blessed the grounds before the dance. Powwows are held often throughout the Southwest, and people of Comanche descent travel great distances to attend them.

Though few in number today, the Comanches are still a distinct and proud people.

GLOSSARY

Bois d'arc A wood (sometimes called Osage orange) favored for making bows and arrows.

Breechclout A piece of cloth worn by men between the legs and belted with loose flaps hanging to the knees front and back.

Buffalo chips Dried buffalo droppings, or feces; was often used for fuel on the Plains.

Comancheria The Spanish name for the area from eastern Colorado and New Mexico to Kansas, Oklahoma, and Texas that was home to the six bands of the Comanche.

Coup stick A lance used to touch a living enemy; considered the highest coup because of the bravery required.

Cradleboard A wooden board used to hold infants. The board could be carried on the mother's back or set upright on the ground.

Lacrosse A ball game played by North America Indian peoples.

Pemmican A favorite food of many Indian peoples; made from buffalo meat mixed with berries, nuts, and animal fat.

Shinny A team ball game played by North American Indian peoples.

Sinew Animal tissue that connects muscle to bone.

Travois A kind of sled tied across the shoulders of a horse, mule, or dog with a family's belongings tied onto parallel poles, the free ends of which drag behind.

FOR FURTHER READING

Lodge, Sally. *The Comanche*. Vero Beach, Fla.: Rourke Publications, 1992.

Mooney, Martin. *The Comanche Indians*. New York: Chelsea House, 1993.

Rollings, Willard H. *The Comanche*. New York: Chelsea House, 1989.

INDEX

ABOUT THE AUTHOR

Judy Alter lives in Texas and writes mostly about the American West. Her other books in the First Book series include *Women of the Old West*, which describes the lives of many different women in the Old West; *Growing Up in the Old West*, which details what life was like for children in the days of the wagon train and the sod hut; and many works of fiction; and *Eli Whitney*, a biography of the famous inventor.

Ms. Alter lives in Fort Worth, Texas; she is the mother of four grown children.